PETER BROWN

WITH THE
ROYAL GEOGRAPHICAL SOCIETY

BRUNEI
Rainforest
Adventure

SPECIAL PHOTOGRAPHY BY
CHRIS CALDICOTT

Universiti Brunei Darussalam –
Royal Geographical Society
Brunei Rainforest Project 1991–92

BBC BOOKS

BRUNEI
Rainforest
Adventure

is printed on environmentally friendly paper.

THE AUTHOR

Peter Brown is a film director on Blue Peter where he produces many of the
programme's environmental items. He is a Fellow of the Royal Geographical Society and
a co-author of BBC Books' best-selling *Blue Peter Green Book*.

This book is published to accompany the
television programmes entitled *Rainforest Adventure*
which were first broadcast in 1993
Published by BBC Books
a division of BBC Enterprises Limited
Woodlands, 80 Wood Lane
London W12 0TT

Based on the television programmes produced
for the BBC by Royal Geographical Society Films.

First published in 1993
© Peter Brown 1993
ISBN 0 563 36756 3 hbk
ISBN 0 563 40304 7 pbk
Designed by The Pinpoint Design Company
Set by Goodfellow & Egan Ltd, Cambridge
Printed in Great Britain by Cambus Litho Ltd, East Kilbride
Bound in Great Britain by Charles Letts Ltd, Edinburgh
Colour separation by Dot Gradations, Chelmsford
Printed paper case printed by Belmont Press Ltd, Northampton
Photograph on page 6 Chris Caldicott
© Royal Geographical Society

The Brunei Rainforest Project acknowledges the sponsorship of the following Corporate Patrons:

ROYAL BRUNEI AIRLINES
THE BARING FOUNDATION
DICAM
GREENCARD TRUST
HONGKONG BANK
MORGAN GRENFELL
NOMURA-NIMCO

Contents

The Untouched Wilderness 8

WANTED
Three Young People for the Adventure of a Lifetime 10

Preparing for the Voyage 12

What is Rainforest? 14

Take Care As You Trek 16

First Taste of Brunei 18

Homes on Stilts 20

Into the Forest 22

The Bukit at Dawn 24

Living with the Wild 26

Rainforest Trek 28

Adventure with a Purpose 30

Mind Where You Tread! 32

The Ant Lady 34

Exotic Plant Wonders 36

Is There a Bomoh in the House? 38

The Night the Earth Shook 40

Water World 42

The Secret World 44

Monsters in Miniature 46

Artist in the Forest 48

Heard But Not Seen 50

Rainforest Music 52

The Forest at Night 54

Magic Moments 56

The Bukit at Sunset 58

A Forest for the Future 60

Rainforest Action 62

Index 64

Left to right: Kieran Hebden (artist), Tom Hewlett (musician) and Severine Bernasconi (reporter), who joined the Royal Geographical Society's expedition into the heart of Brunei's rainforest. The three young adventurers are shown against a background of this pristine wilderness.

Tropical forests, and tropical rainforests in particular, are the final frontier for humankind in more ways than one. Our efforts to protect them will not only determine the quality of life and economic security of future generations, but will test to the limit our readiness to cast off the kind of arrogance that has caused such devastating damage to the global environment, and to become the genuine stewards of *all* life on Earth, not just the human bit of it.

HRH The Prince of Wales

Patron of the Brunei Rainforest Project 1991–92

'The Rainforest Lecture', Royal Botanic Gardens, Kew, 1990

The Untouched Wilderness

Picture a place where the sky is filled with black and turquoise butterflies and horn-billed birds swoop among the treetops. Beams of sunlight shine through luxuriant leaves high up in the canopy – the trees are as tall as skyscrapers. A brightly coloured snake slithers through the tangle of vines and among the tree branches you can pick out curiously shaped fern fronds and the green leaves of orchid plants. You are standing in the middle of a tropical rainforest.

The tropical rainforests of South-East Asia are among the richest and loveliest environments anywhere on Earth, and the forests of Brunei Darussalam on the island of Borneo are still in perfect condition, unspoiled by man.

We hear a lot about rainforests and the damage being done to them, but Brunei's forests are a success story. The country has made the decision to limit logging. Trees are felled to provide the timber needed for Brunei's development, but not for export to other countries.

Rainforest 'University'

In March 1991, the Brunei government declared that Batu Apoi rainforest will become a National Park, protected for all time.

This is where the Royal Geographical Society joined forces with the University of Brunei Darussalam to set up the Brunei Rainforest Project. The centrepiece of the project, and the destination for our expedition, is the Kuala Belalong Field Studies Centre built deep in the jungle – a sort of 'university of the rainforest', where scientists can carry out important research into this untouched wilderness. The hope is that this research will help us to understand more about rainforests throughout the world.

▼ Among the wonders in this impenetrable wilderness is rafflesia, the world's largest flower (see p. 37).

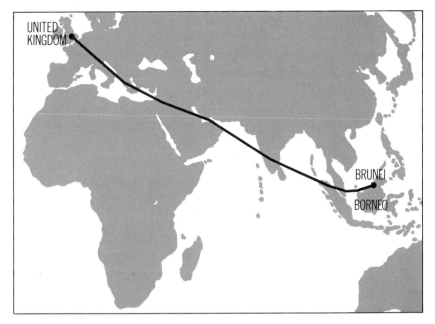

◄ Brunei is a small country in the north-west of the island of Borneo, 11,265 km (7000 miles) from London, in South-East Asia. It is almost entirely covered in lush green tropical forest.

▲ The helmeted hornbill (see p. 51) is one of the millions of plants and animals for which Batu Apoi is home.

◄ 'My mind is a chaos of delight,' wrote the great Victorian naturalist, Charles Darwin, when he first set foot in a tropical rainforest. The Batu Apoi Forest Reserve is steep and mountainous, covered in rich luxuriant vegetation.

▼ The Bornean gibbon depends on the lush green tropical rainforest and spends most of its time up in the trees. In the early morning, gibbon calls can be heard echoing through the forest.

WANTED

Three Young People for the

In 1992, the Royal Geographical Society and the University of Brunei Darussalam invited three young people from Britain to join their rainforest adventure to the Batu Apoi Forest Reserve in Brunei, to see for themselves the scientific work going on in the forest. Their experiences were filmed for two special programmes – *Rainforest Adventure* – screened by BBC Children's Television. In January 1992, Royal Geographical Society Films, who made the programmes, invited schools, colleges, art societies and music groups to nominate young

people for the trip – a two-week, all-expenses-paid expedition to the rainforest in Brunei.

What Does It Take?

'An adventurous spirit, bags of energy and lots of stamina to cope with steep mountainous landscape.' That's what the Royal Geographical Society said it took to be a rainforest adventurer. The treks would be arduous and the young recruits were likely to find themselves stretched to their physical limits. Batu Apoi rainforest is a beautiful

Tom Hewlett
is 14 years old and lives in Chiswick, west London. He is interested in camping and adventure and wants to be a pilot when he leaves school. He once had a flying lesson for a present. Tom's main interest is music and he plays saxophone and clarinet in a band with some friends. He was intrigued by the idea of capturing the mood of the forest in music.

Adventure of a Lifetime

but difficult place in which to work – hot, humid and very tiring. That's why large areas are still unexplored.

The jungle is also fraught with hazards such as thorny creepers and steep slippery trails, but it need not be dangerous if people keep their wits about them. However, it is crawling with insects, large and small, and leeches, so it is not a place for the squeamish!

The expedition was to be more than an endurance test. The idea was to look at the rainforest project through the eyes of young people, so the film crew needed recruits with lively and enquiring minds who would find out about the scientific work and ask challenging questions about the research going on at the Kuala Belalong Field Studies Centre.

They were also looking for people who could put across their experiences and feelings in pictures, words and music, to capture the spirit of the rainforest.

A short-list was drawn up and, after interviews, three young people were selected. This is the story of their adventure to Brunei's pristine rainforest.

Severine Bernasconi
is 13 years old and lives in Hucknall, Nottinghamshire. She is very keen on the outdoor life and enjoys sailing, canoeing and walking her dog. Hucknall is in the heart of Robin Hood country and Severine has been involved in a scheme to replant Nottinghamshire's lost forest. She also enjoys interviewing people and writing articles. One of them appeared in a national newspaper.

Kieran Hebden
is 14 years old and lives in south London. His hobby is sketching and painting; on Sunday afternoons he can often be seen with his sketch-pad along the river Thames. He enjoys all forms of art and that includes an enormous collection of model soldiers which he has hand-painted. He was keen to develop his skills at painting landscapes and looked forward to the challenge of depicting the rainforest.

Preparing for the Voyage

The first stage for the rainforest adventurers was to visit the doctor for inoculations against diseases which can be picked up in the jungle. The doctor accessed Brunei on a computer which has updated information about diseases all over the world. No need for vaccination against yellow fever, but typhoid, yes, polio, yes . . . No malaria is recorded in Brunei at the moment, but the Royal Geographical Society advised everyone to take anti-malarial precautions anyway because not enough is known about the state of the disease in the remote part of the jungle in which the Centre is situated.

The next thing to prepare was kit. The RGS's Expedition Advisory Centre had a list.

Rucksacks with lots of side pockets would be easier to carry than suitcases on the longer journeys. They suggested a small one for short treks and a larger one to take clothing and equipment to and from camp.

Resealable polythene bags and lots of them! Sooner or later everything will get drenched, either by the rain or in the river, so clothes and documents have to be protected. Kieran sealed his art materials in a waterproof box and Tom kept his saxophone case in a polythene bag.

Light clothing including two shirts (long-sleeved), T-shirts, baggy trousers and socks.

An **'Indiana Jones-style' bush hat** to protect against the blazing sun during the river journey.

A **towel** or **sarong** (which we could buy in Brunei). A sarong is the traditional wrap-around garment in Brunei, very practical to use either as an easy-to-dry towel or cool clothing.

Desert boots or **lightweight walking boots** for the rough terrain, **deck shoes** for the river journey to the Kuala Belalong Centre.

The Expedition Advisory Centre also listed items to take in the small rucksack.

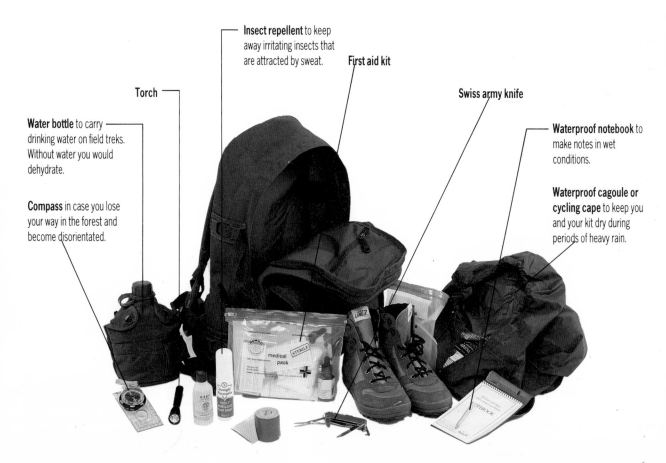

Insect repellent to keep away irritating insects that are attracted by sweat.

First aid kit

Torch

Swiss army knife

Water bottle to carry drinking water on field treks. Without water you would dehydrate.

Compass in case you lose your way in the forest and become disorientated.

Waterproof notebook to make notes in wet conditions.

Waterproof cagoule or cycling cape to keep you and your kit dry during periods of heavy rain.

▶ David Bellamy shows Severine, Tom and Kieran the wonders of the rainforest that can be seen in the Palm House at London's Kew Gardens (main photograph). Every plant has a story to tell.

London's Rainforest

If you want to get a taste of what it is like to be in a tropical rainforest without actually being there, the best place to go is Kew Gardens in London. The Palm House is like all the world's rainforests rolled into one and this is where Tom, Severine and Kieran got a few last-minute tips from top botanist David Bellamy.

David explained that the Palm House represents the top layer of the forest. Underground heaters and sprinklers keep the atmosphere hot and very humid and everyone soon started to sweat. David showed the way rainforest plants have adapted to their conditions – 'drip tips' on leaves are an example – and pointed out some of the many useful plants like bamboo and bananas that grow in rainforests. He also warned everyone about sitting on ant plants (see p. 35).

What is Rainforest?

Rainforests are among the richest and least explored environments on Earth. It isn't hard to discover a new species of animal or plant as you trek through one of them. Look under rotting tree stumps, sift through leaf litter and peer into pools and you'll spot hundreds of strange life forms. The chances are at least one of them will never have been named by science.

In Batu Apoi rainforest, an area not much larger than a football field can have over 150 species of tree, 90 species of ground-living plants and thousands of species of insect! New discoveries are being made all the time. Wherever you look there is life. The keyword is 'biodiversity' – the richness of species and life forms. Why rainforests harbour so many types of plants and animals is one of the great mysteries being researched by the Brunei Rainforest Project.

Tropical rainforests lie in a band around the Equator and are both warm and wet. More than 2 metres (6 ft) of rain falls in a single year and there are no sharp differences between the seasons. The forests are very old. They took thousands of years to establish and plants and animals have adapted to fill every niche. You couldn't duplicate a rainforest in a glasshouse. Once gone it would take thousands of years before it was established again.

The Batu Apoi rainforest is dominated by giant dipterocarp trees, some of them over 30 metres (100 ft) high – the height of a 15-storey building. Huge buttress roots support them and ground roots snake out across the forest floor.

The struggle for light

Most living things in the rainforest are found in the canopy. There is intense competition between the smaller trees and the young 'kings of the forest' (the tallest trees) to get at the light. Snakes, squirrels, monkeys and many birds live in the canopy.

To get nearer to the sunlight many plants, called 'epiphytes', grow directly on the branches of trees instead of on the forest floor.

As you get lower down it gets darker and gloomier – only 2 per cent of the sunlight reaches the ground. This is the domain of young seedlings and plants like ferns and gingers that can tolerate low light.

Take Care As You Trek

Trekking through the jungle, you have to be careful where you tread and what you touch. The black sap of the rengas tree causes a serious rash if you come in contact with it. If you want to rest awhile on a branch or tree stump, it is best to tap the bark first to make sure it isn't crawling with ants.

When it rains, the forest floor and undergrowth are infested with leeches, whose senses are alert, waiting for passing animals. Leeches get through socks and clothing and stick to skin where they suck blood. They are an occupational hazard for anyone working in the jungle. People just pull them off gently and, most of the time, don't even notice they've been bitten until they find the red stain on their shirt!

▶ **When a tree comes tumbling down**
When an old tree dies and crashes to the ground, it creates a break in the canopy, letting in the sunlight. Seeds, dormant in the soil for many years, germinate, while the crop of young trees in the understorey beneath the canopy bursts into life as light and rainwater reach them, causing vigorous growth straight upwards. Meanwhile, microbes, termites, beetles and fungi eat away and rot the dead tree, gradually releasing nutrients to make new plant food. Nothing goes to waste. Everything is recycled by nature.

Eventually, the new growth of trees and other plants from the surrounding forest re-colonises the clearing. Over many years, it repairs the hole in the canopy.

▼ A strange and startling display for the jungle traveller – flowers and fruits that grow straight from the trunks of trees. Here they are openly exposed to animals that will pollinate and disperse them.

Curiouser and Curiouser
Curious life forms are everywhere. Creepers with rope-like stems hang from the branches of trees and flowers display a habit called 'cauliflory' where they grow straight from the trunks. The free space beneath the canopy layer high above your head is buzzing with the insects and bats that pollinate flowers and feed on fruits.

▶ This strangler fig developed from a seed that germinated high up on the branch of the tree. The plant sent down roots and became bigger. Eventually, it will envelope the trunk and kill the tree leaving the strangler fig tree in its place.

First Taste of Brunei

Through the window of the Boeing 757, the forest stretched as far as the eye could see – a carpet of green broken only by meandering rivers. It was the end of an 18-hour flight which had taken the team over mountains, oceans, deserts and, finally, the rainforests of Borneo, 11,265 km (7000 miles) from home.

As Severine, Tom and Kieran stepped, jet-lagged and a little shaky, on to the tarmac at Bandar Seri Begawan, Brunei's capital, they felt their first blast of the country's sweltering heat. Everyone adjusted their watches. Brunei is 8 hours ahead of United Kingdom time, so while friends at home were going to bed, they were just starting the next day!

Bandar Seri Begawan (or BSB as it's known) is on the shores of the Brunei River on the north-west tip of Borneo. Dominating its skyline is the gold dome of the Omar Ali Saiffudin Mosque. A loudspeaker perched on its minaret sounds the call to prayer: Brunei is a Muslim country and its people live by Islamic rules.

With its Italian marble, Venetian-style mosaics and stained-glass windows, the Omar Ali. Saiffudin Mosque is a monument to Islam.

▲ Kieran's sketch of a replica of a sixteenth-century royal barge that stands in a man-made lagoon circling the mosque.

S E V E R I N E ' S   D I A R Y

The golden dome of the mosque sparkled in the sun – what an impressive building. The floor on which we walked was decorated with beautiful tile patterns. One of the most pleasant places was the pool of rainwater where people go to wash their hands and feet before entering the mosque.

Homes on Stilts

Many Bruneians prefer traditional homes to city apartments and 30,000 of them live in the Kampong Ayer, the world's largest water village where the houses are built on stilts. More than a collection of homes, it is a whole community, complete with shops, a mosque, schools, a medical centre and even a fire station.

When the tide is high people go in boats to sell their wares, and in the early morning rush-hour water taxis zoom around the stilted houses taking commuters to work. The Kampong Ayer is by no means a shanty town on the edge of the city. The houses are spacious and modern inside. Everyone has a television and stereo and most families have a gleaming white car on the mainland. Brunei has more cars per head of population than anywhere else in the world!

People prefer to live in the water village because they can be close to friends and relatives. Many families have lived in the Kampong Ayer for generations.

Everything in BSB comes and goes by boat. A bustling market is the link between the town and the rainforest – many of the fruits you can buy there have their origins in the jungle.

◄ Oozing with oil!
'I smell oil', said an employee of Shell in 1903 while lying on the beach in Brunei. He was sitting on a giant reservoir of oil which later made the country rich. Today, 'nodding donkey' oil wells like this one make Brunei a major oil producer.

▼ In the shadow of the Omar Ali Saiffudin Mosque, extending from both shores of the Brunei River, is the Kampong Ayer, recognised as the world's largest water village. Taking a boat journey around the labyrinth of creeks and water lanes is like stepping back in time.

SEVERINE'S DIARY

The low morning light made the kampong Ayer look dark and mysterious. A labyrinth of walkways lay in front of me, with colourful flowers, the smells of exotic cooking and the sounds of cats and chickens. It felt as though I was stepping back in time.

Into the Forest

Leaving the city of Bandar Seri Begawan behind them, the team set off on the long journey up the Temburong River into the rainforest. The first leg of the voyage was by a taxi with a difference: a powerboat took them on a 40-minute ride through the mangrove swamps to Bangar, a small but busy town on the edge of the forest. Like any other Bruneian town, Bangar has buses, lorries, mosques and shops. What is amazing is that it is completely cut off from the western part of Brunei by road – everything from there reaches it by boat.

Mud, mud, glorious mud!
Half-metre (20 in) long mudcrunching worms, horseshoe crabs – the survivors of a lost world – crocodiles and rare proboscis monkeys. These are the creatures of Brunei's mangrove swamps, the tentacles of forest that stretch out on to the coastal mudflats. It is an eerie and secret world, difficult to penetrate. It is also a naturalist's dream. Here you can see mudskipper fish that climb trees, and observe monitor lizards like leftovers from the days of the dinosaurs, whose forked tongues dart in and out.

We climbed into the longboats and began to power our way up the Temburong River. When the water was too strong for the engine there was only one thing for it — get out and push. The current rushing past my legs is an experience I'll never forget. We were all completely soaked.

▼ Into the forest the fast way: a powerboat water taxi takes our adventurers on a high-speed ride through mysterious mangrove swamps on their journey into the jungle.

▶ The final leg of the journey into the forest was by motorised longboat up the Temburong rapids. When the torrent became too strong the team had to climb into the water and push!

◀ The fish that climbs trees! The mudskipper is only a few centimetres long, but it has developed a way of edging itself out of the water and up the trunks of trees using its front fins. It breathes by taking in oxygen from the water it holds in its mouth.

The Bukit at Dawn

At 900 metres (2995 ft) the Bukit (which is Malay for 'hill') is the highest point of the Batu Apoi Forest Reserve. From its summit, the view of the rainforest stretches many kilometres into neighbouring Sarawak.

24

Living with the Wild

Hidden away among the dense foliage on the slopes of a steep gorge along the Belalong River is Kuala Belalong Field Studies Centre. For over a year this has been the base camp of the Brunei Rainforest Project – a research station deep in the jungle where scientists are trying to answer questions that could explain the complex biology of the rainforests.

From the landing-stage by the river, a system of walkways joins six wooden buildings. One of them is a dining-room with a kitchen and one is a fully equipped field laboratory where scientists are hard at work on their projects. Four accommodation houses can take up to 30 people – at a squeeze!

Snapshot of Camp

In the laboratory, Ruth Levy examines her collections of forest ants and Alan Dykes prepares soil samples from a recent landslide. John Wills enters the mountain of new data on to the computer database.

Through the window, the team can see other scientists with bulging rucksacks leaving the camp to go on research treks. By the river the boatmen prepare the longboats for a journey upstream.

Meanwhile, in the kitchen, the cook prepares a Malaysian rice dish for the scientists staying at the camp. The whir of the generator that produces 'mains' electricity is drowned by a symphony of cicadas.

Environment-friendly

The research station is designed to blend in with the jungle without harming it. The wooden walkways stop soil being eroded away. The Centre's own mini-sewerage works ensures that the water pumped from the river for showers, cooking – and even flush toilets – is purified before going back into the river. Empty cans, packaging and rubbish are taken away to be disposed of in Bangar.

◀ You never know where you are going to encounter wildlife at the Centre. A large millipede like this one (shown curled up) was seen creeping across the kitchen floor!

Tropical Home from Home

Lizards can be seen running around the walkways, fruit bats roost under the leaf of a banana tree. The sky is alive with butterflies. The Centre makes a perfect wildlife observatory. In many ways staying here is like a home from home, but with a few differences.

The laundry is the river (using environment-friendly washing powder of course), but, because the atmosphere is so humid, it can take days for clothes to dry. It is tempting to wear the same wet garments for days on end for trekking – except that they go mouldy. The trick is to wash clothes in the morning, leave them to dry in the hot sunshine, and to take them in before the evening rain.

Putting your boots on in the morning is another ritual. First you have to wipe off the bees attracted by the sweat, then turn them upside down to check for scorpions.

Unlike in Africa, there are no lions at night – just millions of creepy-crawlies. Once you get used to giant beetles and stick insects Kuala Belalong is paradise on Earth.

◀ The Field Studies Centre, painted by Kieran. Six buildings made from local timber are home for the project's scientists.

▼ Animals shared the adventurers' home from home. Severine is very fond of them, but with no cats or dogs to stroke at camp she had to make friends with this enormous beetle which she found in her room.

◀ Paradise on Earth – the destination for the rainforest adventure was the Kuala Belalong Field Studies Centre. It is built in a woody gorge on the banks of a river deep in the heart of the Batu Apoi Forest Reserve.

◀ Beautiful butterflies like this colourful birdwing flutter around the houses at Kuala Belalong. On the rocks in a gentle stream alongside the camp they gather in their hundreds.

Rainforest Trek

'It's one of the richest and most diverse environments on Earth – so where's all the wildlife?' That was the team's immediate reaction on their first trek into the rainforest. It was only when they took a second look through the dense foliage and paid attention to detail that they realised they were surrounded by creepy-crawlies. Most animals are timid and well camouflaged.

Lord Cranbrook, leader of the Brunei Rainforest Project, had led them over the swaying rope bridge across the river into the mysterious world beyond. The terrain was steep and rugged and the going tough. The air was still and humid and sweat poured off everyone in the team. Every few minutes they had to stop for a drink of water or they would have risked becoming dehydrated.

After an exhausting trek, the team arrived at this trickle of water running over a rock – the head of a newly discovered waterfall, hidden deep in the forest.

▶ Wherever you look there is life. The forest is alive with insects like this huge beetle, sketched by Kieran.

SEVERINE'S DIARY

The plant life was totally different to anything I'd ever seen before. Flowers grew from the tree trunks and black and red sap poured from the wood. I was tempted to wander off to look at things, but Lord Cranbrook warned us not to stray or we'd get lost. The forest wasn't as scary as I'd imagined.

Adventure with a Purpose

Shooting rapids, following trails through thick jungle, camping out in leech-infested undergrowth . . . The Brunei Rainforest Project is as exciting as any *Indiana Jones* adventure – but it's adventure with an important purpose. The Kuala Belalong Field Studies Centre is at its heart, making Brunei's rainforest accessible so that scientists can work in the forest and search out its secrets.

Tropical Treasure Chests
Rainforests are one of Earth's important tropical environments, yet logging and clear-felling are said to take an area the size of Iceland every year.

They are a treasure chest of plants, animals and chemicals that could benefit mankind, and their broad-leaved trees regulate our atmosphere and climate by absorbing carbon dioxide from the air and releasing oxygen. The loss of Earth's rainforests does not only put their riches at risk; it may also injure the 'lungs' of our planet.

One aim of the Brunei Rainforest Project is to find new uses for the plants of the forest, especially medicinal ones that can be harvested without destroying their environment – to show that the forests are worth more standing up than they are cut down as logs.

Scientists and Surveys

Over the next few days Tom, Severine and Kieran met some of the scientists who are working at Kuala Belalong.

Dr Satish Choy is a freshwater biologist, studying life in the rainforest's rivers. Using traditional fish nets, he has so far found freshwater crabs, 19 species of fish, and six species of prawn – one of them previously unknown to science. He has found loaches that stick to rocks in the rapids and change colour to blend in with the background. Loaches don't like it when the water gets muddy so Satish thinks they could be living indicators of the state of rainforest rivers. Maybe they could be used to measure the silting effects of land clearance or logging.

◀ The one that didn't get away! Tom casts a net into the river to help Dr Satish Choy with his research into the biology of the rainforest's rivers.

▲ Dr Joe Charles catches and examines mammals to discover more about their movements through the forest.

▲ Research assistant John Wills enters the mountain of eco-data collected by scientists on to the Centre's computer. The Geographical Information System is a way of recording information so that it can be used and updated by scientists working at Kuala Belalong in the future.

Dr Joe Charles uses harmless traps to catch ground-dwelling and understorey mammals, which he anaesthetises, gently examines, then returns unharmed to the wild. Through his research he is finding out about their diets, growth and movements.

Scientists collecting samples or carrying out surveys have to know precisely where they are in the forest if their work is to be of use, so a sophisticated satellite navigation system is used to pinpoint their position. The results of scientific surveys are fed into the computer-based Geographical Information System. Like a complicated jigsaw puzzle, GIS is gradually building up a picture of the forest, piece by piece.

TOM'S DIARY

Satish showed me how to use the net without getting it tangled. My throw turned out to be more of a chuck than a skilful sling, but to my astonishment it worked – I caught a fascinating fish which kept changing colour.

Mind Where You Tread!

There's a sign at the Centre which reads: 'Beware – in the forest look out for snakes on paths and low vegetation, often well camouflaged. Snakes are found at Camp. They have been seen on walkways and under the houses.'

Of all the animals in the forest, snakes conjure up the greatest fears. People imagine that the jungle is full of them and that their sole aim in life is to attack anyone who ventures into their world. In practice, they are rarely seen in the forest. Most are very timid and slither away the moment they hear footsteps.

Snake Facts

Some snakes live high up in trees where they hunt their prey: frogs, small mammals and birds. There are even flying ones that glide from tree to tree.

Although most snakes encountered in the jungle are small, there are rare, monster-sized specimens. Snakes have few enemies, and when food is plentiful and they are undisturbed they often reach their full size, however small (or large) that may be.

There are some dangerous snakes in Brunei like the deadly king cobra and the python, and you need to watch out in case you accidentally corner one. Most people bitten by snakes in Brunei suffer negligible venom. Even a lethal dose generally takes hours or days, not seconds or minutes, to have an effect so there should be time to get the patient flown to a hospital.

▼ Snake expert Dr Indraneil Das has been studying where snakes live in the forest and catches them by hand. Yes, he has been bitten, but so far he has not suffered any ill effects.

Brunei's deadliest snake
e bite of the king cobra is enough to kill
elephant. Indraneil says there is an
i-serum, but sometimes the cobra
inject so much venom – about a
lespoonful – that there is no cure.
ckily, its natural diet is other snakes!

▲ Animal-eaters
Brunei's largest snake was a 6.5 metre (21½ ft)
reticulated python – a longer version of the one
shown in this photograph. It was spotted in 1979
and shot by soldiers. Eight men were needed to
carry it: its average girth was 45 cm (1½ ft) and
it weighed 90 kg (200 lb). There was a huge
bulge in its stomach which turned out to be the
remains of a barking deer, complete with antlers.
How many more giant snakes are lurking in the
undergrowth?

The Ant Lady

Ruth Levy has one big passion in life: ants! Most people think of them as insect pests, but to Ruth they are the pinnacle of evolution.

For the last 12 months she has given up the comforts of her Oxford home to crawl through the undergrowth, getting bitten to pieces, to study ants. She has found over 200 types in the forest, so she has a lot to write home abou

Ruth is researching ants to discover how they forage for food and why there are so many different types. She goes ant watching and lures them with her favourite ant recipes: sugared water and tuna fish – dolphin-friendly, needless to say!

▶ Mind where you sit!

Termites are not ants – they are more closely related to cockroaches – but, like ants, they play an important role in the rainforest. They help dead tree-strumps and leaf litter to decompose.

On the forest trees you can see huge 'termite motorways' like this one where they carry food back to their nests. The soldiers don't have jaws, but each one has a small pointed gland on its head which it uses as a chemical weapon to squirt an unpleasant liquid!

The Super-organism

Ants are the most common animals in the rainforest – they make up about 70 per cent of the living things there. Ruth says they are successful because they are so well organised. There is no such thing as a solitary ant. They work in groups and their social behaviour is so advanced that, although they are divided into queens, workers and soldiers, they act as one big organism.

One species of ant finds protection in a kind of rattan palm. If you lean on one of these 'ant plants' the ants will tap it with their jaws to make a hiss, then shoot out and attack you.

▼ The biggest ant in Brunei is Camponotus gigas – Ruth calls it 'campo'. The soldiers are the size of 10p pieces!

◀ Spot the ant! Armed with a magnifier, Ruth Levy goes ant-watching in the undergrowth. Her techniques for studying ants include marking them with blobs of paint so that she can pinpoint the movements of individual ants in the colony.

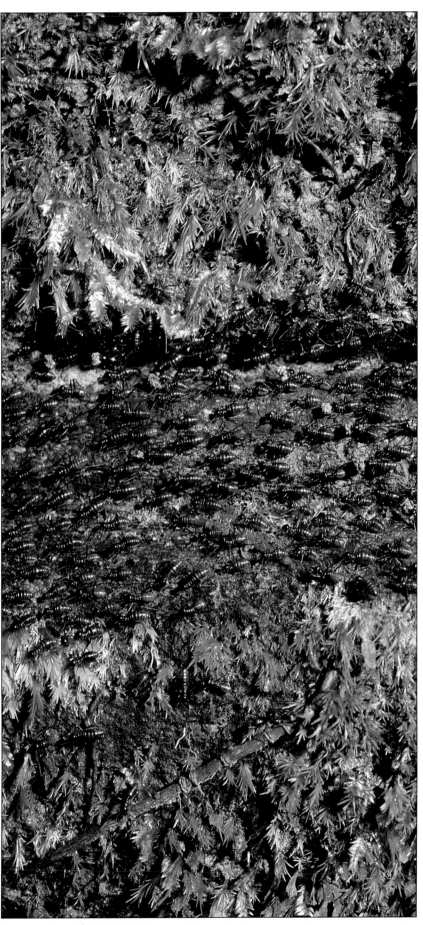

Exotic Plant Wonders

Brunei is home for some of the most fascinating plants in the world. The struggle for light, nutrients and water has created a richness of unusual forms and the jungle is a bewildering mass of ferns, towering trees, vines and flowers. There are no seasons in the forest. Day-length and temperature are almost the same all year round, and the wet and dry seasons are irregular and unpredictable.

▶ The insect eaters

Many jungle habitats are poor in plant nutrients, so pitcher plants have developed an ingenious way of feeding: they eat insects. They are shaped like funnels with downward-pointing spines inside the rims. The lid of the pitcher exudes nectar which attracts insects. At the bottom of the funnel is an 'enzyme soup' that dissolves flies unfortunate enough to fall in.

Not all creatures are killed by the pitcher's enzymes – some small frogs and mosquito larvae thrive blissfully in the funnels. The plants have become mini-habitats in themselves. There are many species of pitchers. The plants are most commonly found on poor soils and, especially, mountain ridges. Many are climbers.

▲ Delicacy and decay

In the midst of death there is life! The jungle is constantly changing as trees grow up then topple over. It is the fungi that recycle the mess. They play an important role in the rainforest because they help dead timber and leaves to rot and make new plant food. Some of the weirdest looking plants in the forest are fungi. Knowledge about their adaptations is in its infancy – why they grow into such strange and delicate shapes is still a mystery.

The jungle was alive with incredible plants. Everywhere you look another weird and wonderful kind of plant hits you in the face – from the most beautiful flowers to glow-in-the-dark mushrooms. The trees in the jungle are enormous and I felt very small amongst them.

▶ Rainforest harvest

Rainforests are the source of some of our most useful plants, like bananas, bamboo, cocoa and potatoes. Many food plants started as wild species in the jungle. Most are now cultivated in plantations, but their wild ancestors still have an important role to play. Infusions of genetic material from them improve crop yields and increase resistance to disease and pests. The forest is an enormous 'gene bank' which commercial growers can turn to when they need to replenish their stock.

◀ The world's largest flower

One of the rare and most curious plants in Brunei is the rafflesia, a parasite whose flower can be over a metre (3 ft) across. It doesn't have a stem, leaves or true roots, just a gaudily speckled giant flower that grows directly from the stem of the vine on which it lives. It is so rare and so little understood that nobody knows whether it is pollinated by ants or other insects. You would imagine that such a huge flower would have a beautiful scent but it actually smells of rotting beef!

Is There a Bomoh in the House?

When people get sick in the jungle they often ask to see the local bomoh, or medicine man. The bomoh uses herbal remedies prepared from rainforest plants – wisdom that has been handed down over the generations.

Jungle medicine might seem like folklore and superstition, but many rainforest remedies have a scientific basis. Fierce competition in the struggle to survive has created a wealth of chemicals, locked away in leaves, roots or shoots, which the forest plants use for defence, attraction and repulsion. The healing potential of these chemicals is well known to medicine men.

▼ Kieran (bottom right), Dr Kamariah (left) and the local medicine man (centre) go hunting for medicinal plants which grow on the floor of the rainforest.

Rainforest Remedies

Amoebic dysentery is cured with a rainforest plant, the ipecac, and quinine, a chemical from the bark of the cinchona tree, was the first preventative and cure for malaria.

Cancer is now under attack by rainforest drugs – 70 per cent of the 3000 plants identified by United States scientists as having 'anti-cancer' properties come from rainforests.

The active ingredients in one-quarter of all prescription drugs in our chemist shops originated in tropical rainforests. There must be many more waiting to be discovered. The search is on in the hope that cures for the world's worst diseases, like Aids, will one day be found among the forest plants.

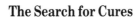

Could a cure for Aids be hidden among the plants in Kieran's painting? The jungle is a chemical treasure chest, full of secrets.

The Search for Cures

Loya anak Kaling is a local medicine man and has a lifelong knowledge of the jungle. His potions, which he prepares from rainforest plants, include cures for stomach-ache, diarrhoea, rashes, toothache, boils and jaundice. If a child comes to him with stomach-ache he applies the bark of a 'buhau' tree to the outside of the stomach. He uses the leaves of another plant to treat coughs and its roots to cure headaches.

Dr Kamariah Abu Salim goes plant hunting with the local medicine men. She is researching the chemical background behind their potions. Loya takes her on treks deep into the jungle and shows her the plants he uses. She asks him the plant's local name, then records how he prepares and applies his remedy. She then collects a specimen of the plant and takes it for chemical analysis. That way she hopes to find the active ingredients in his cures.

So far, through her research, Dr Kamariah has identified 79 plants that have medicinal uses. Maybe some of Loya's rainforest potions will be developed into pharmaceuticals and find their way on to our chemists' shelves.

▼ Mucuna is a rainforest plant which produces a chemical used in the treatment of Parkinson's Disease.

The Night the Earth Shook

It started with a violent thunderstorm followed by days of torrential rain. Water pouring through the canopy gushed into the Temburong River, which rose 2 metres (6½ ft) and turned brown with sediment.

Over a long period of time, the river had been eating away at the side of a steep gorge. Then, that day about 30 years ago, according to the local people, there was an enormous rumble like an earthquake, and the crash of giant dipterocarp trees tumbling off the cliff. The base of the gorge had snapped off and trees, rock and soil plunged into the waters below leaving a chasm. Fortunately, no one was under the cliff at the time, but when people returned they found a scene of complete devastation: a huge landslide. The gorge would never be the same again.

Landslides and Water Ways

Landslides are a common feature of Batu Apoi's steep forest terrain. They are just one part of the complicated cycle of life which makes this rainforest so rich.

Geographer Alan Dykes hopes that the work he is doing, using 'yoghurt pot' science techniques, will enable him to predict which areas are likely to suffer landslides in the future. By comparing the way water flows through plots with trees and plots with exposed soil, he is also showing why deforestation causes massive land erosion. Alan likes rain because it fills his bottles and measuring-jugs and helps him study the way water moves through the forest.

◄ **Studying the soil**

Alan Dykes stands in one of his soil pits. The photograph shows just how shallow rainforest soil is. If the fragile 10 cm (4 in) or so of topsoil is washed away, absolutely nothing grows on the bare rock and clay left below. Cutting down trees can soon turn a rainforest into a desert. Millions of people throughout the world are now suffering the effects of erosion caused by deforestation.

▶ 'Where landslides destroy habitats, nature creates new ones,' says Alan Dykes. Landslides are soon colonised by invading plants and animals – they add to the richness of the forest by helping to create a patchwork of habitats.

Water World

Water is the dominant force in the rainforest. Rivers rise and fall 2 or 3 metres (6 or 9 ft) overnight and the action of water on the forest's soft shales creates beautiful waterfalls which are carved out of the mountainside. Each one is a miniature world for thousands of animals and plants.

The Secret World

Most of what happens in the rainforest goes on 30–40 metres (98–130 ft) above our heads, in the secret world of the canopy. Most of the forest's birds and mammals live up there among the tangle of foliage and epiphytic plants. Some frogs spend their whole lives in pools of rainwater between the branches. The only way to see them is to climb up to them.

There are insect-eating plants which are never seen on the forest floor. Rare mammals move along aerial highways, invisible from the ground.

The only chance most people have to see the plants of the canopy in close-up is when a tree falls down. This is frustrating for rainforest scientists as it is important for them to get a complete picture of how the forest works.

Climb to the Canopy

Researching the canopy is the job of the tree climbers. To climb really tall trees they use ropes and tackle because the ascent is fraught with danger. Branches are wet and slippery and, unlike when climbing a mountain, they are likely to come face to face with large insects and snakes slithering down towards them.

The route has to be as carefully planned as if they were climbing a rock face. Unhealthy trees have to be avoided, so do wasps' nests! Once on the canopy an undiscovered world opens up to the aerial explorer. Scientists can have intimate contact with animals and plants that are never visible from the ground.

At Kuala Belalong researchers have been climbing trees to collect insects and study leaf forms. Most of the world may have been explored at ground level, but the jungle canopy is still as little explored as the ocean depths.

▶ Reaching the tantalising canopy gardens is the work of the tree climbers. Using techniques borrowed from mountaineers, scientists are now able to research even the remotest parts of the rainforest roof, where most of the animals live.

▶ **Inflatable observatory**
In Brunei scientists are proposing to use air platforms like this one in French Guiana. The huge inflatable lilos rest gently on the canopy. Researchers get to them by balloon.

In other rainforests, scientists have built observatories on towers of scaffolding. In South America some researchers constructed a labyrinth of aerial walkways in the canopy – like Robin Hood's hide-away in the film *Prince of Thieves*. In Panama, they even erected a tower crane so that scientists could swoop down on to the canopy in a gondola.

Monsters in Miniature

Think of the squidgiest, hairiest, bug-eyed monster of your worst nightmare. It probably already exists in miniature in a tropical rainforest!

The curious adaptations of jungle creatures are as fearsome as any of the horrors dreamt up by science fiction writers. There are multi-eyed spiders that can see in every direction, insects that look like flowers, giant centipedes, rhinoceros-shaped beetles, fish that change colour and even animals that glow in the dark.

In their struggle to survive in the hostile jungle, creatures have evolved weird and wonderful shapes and colours – elaborate camouflages that help them go unnoticed.

▲ Colourful creatures

Not all creatures try to hide themselves. Some, like this coral snake, have bright colours to warn other animals that they are poisonous or have a nasty sting if attacked. Some harmless creatures protect themselves by mimicking the colours and shapes of wasps and poisonous snakes. Their survival is a game of bluff.

Many birds are brightly coloured to attract a mate of the same species. Because they can escape easily and have only few predators, birds don't need camouflage. Some of the most beautiful birds in the world are found in the rainforests.

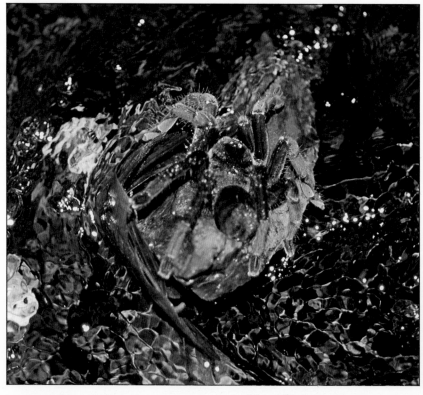

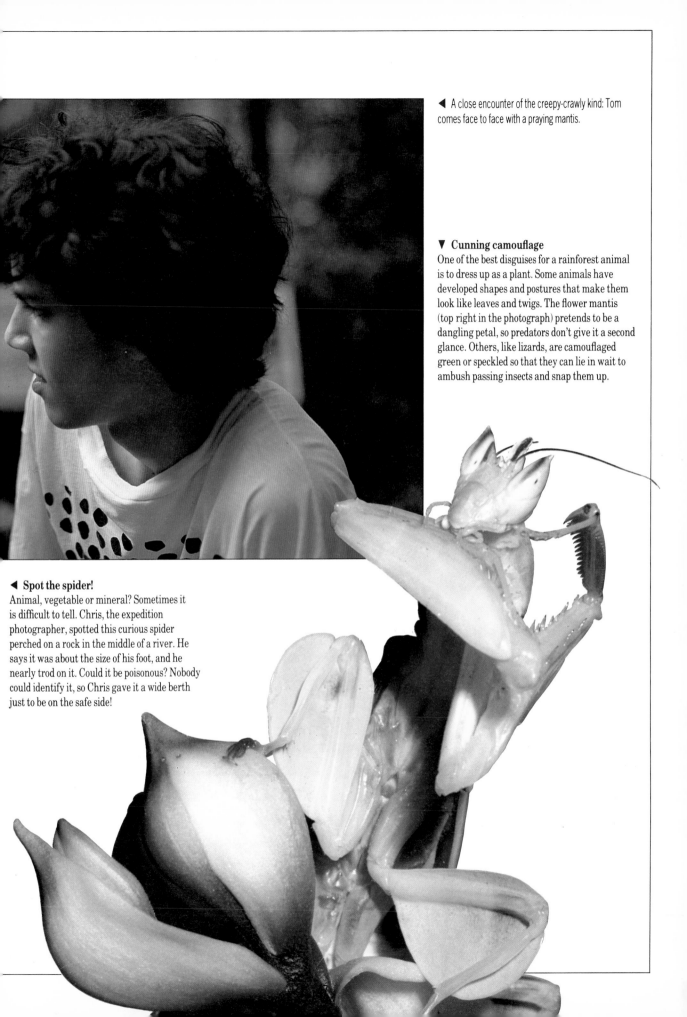

◀ A close encounter of the creepy-crawly kind: Tom comes face to face with a praying mantis.

▼ Cunning camouflage

One of the best disguises for a rainforest animal is to dress up as a plant. Some animals have developed shapes and postures that make them look like leaves and twigs. The flower mantis (top right in the photograph) pretends to be a dangling petal, so predators don't give it a second glance. Others, like lizards, are camouflaged green or speckled so that they can lie in wait to ambush passing insects and snap them up.

◀ Spot the spider!

Animal, vegetable or mineral? Sometimes it is difficult to tell. Chris, the expedition photographer, spotted this curious spider perched on a rock in the middle of a river. He says it was about the size of his foot, and he nearly trod on it. Could it be poisonous? Nobody could identify it, so Chris gave it a wide berth just to be on the safe side!

Artist in the Forest

The artist has traditionally been an important member of an expedition. Before the days of cameras he or she was there to record discoveries and important moments. A sketch-pad isn't the same as a camera. It records a scene the way the artist sees it, rather than being a detailed snapshot of how it actually is. In the past, expedition art was often used to make the landscape more atmospheric – or even to make the explorer look more heroic!

An artist can communicate a mood or a feeling about a place in a way that the camera cannot. This is what Kieran has done with his paintings. He has captured the bewildering richness of the rainforest as he saw it.

▶ In a pool of light among the ferns and creepers, Kieran captures the atmosphere of the rainforest in a sketch. Surrounded by a myriad of shapes and colours, he is not left short of inspiration.

KIERAN'S DIARY

Painting the forest is more complicated than it seems. Because there is so much humidity it is hard to keep the paper dry. I had to be careful in case my pictures got ruined. Another problem is rain. As soon as I got outside and started painting it would rain. I longed for my desk in a dry room!

Heard But Not Seen

'You can't see the wood for the trees.' This phrase takes on a new meaning in a tropical rainforest. Because the undergrowth is so dense, you can see only a few metres in each direction and most mammals and birds are difficult to spot. The majority of large animals lie low and bolt when they hear people coming. You hear them more often than you see them.

Most activity goes on in the canopy where flying squirrels leap from branch to branch and even lizards have wings and glide from tree to tree. Monkeys are difficult to see, but they can be heard crashing through the treetops.

▶ Porcupines range the forest floor, feeding on fallen fruits. They are especially fond of durians.

▼ More often heard crashing through the canopy than seen, the Bornean gibbon is a spectacular aerial acrobat. It uses its 'suspensory' posture, seen here, to get around the treetops and reach ripe fruit at the very ends of branches.

▲ A rare sight in the Batu Apoi Rainforest, the Malayan sun bear is the smallest member of the bear family. It spends a lot of its time resting, or feeding in the trees on fruits, termites, small mammals and even birds.

Hornbill
A sound like rushing air high up in the trees, then the flapping of large wings is the sign of a hornbill. The hornbill is one of the world's rarest birds. Very timid, it spends most of its time in the dense canopy.

Its strange bill may seem cumbersome, but it is a very useful tool. It enables the hornbill to reach fruits that would otherwise be hanging out of reach, and to catch prey such as small birds and squirrels. Like the beak of a woodpecker, it is also good for digging into soft wood to reach insects.

Jungle Detective

The rainforest researcher has to use all the ingenuity of a detective to study mammals and birds. One way is to lie in wait in a clearing, or on an animal trail, armed with a pair of binoculars or a camera. Another is to set harmless traps and nets.

Most information comes from animal tracks and signs. At a waterhole half-way down a slope there are footprints in the mud, perhaps a sign that a barking deer or a Malayan sun bear is in the area. Among rotting leaves, a grey stick turns out to be the spine of a porcupine.

The noises animals make are also a give-away. Frogs, birds, insects and mammals have their own distinctive sounds that tell researchers a particular animal is out there in the jungle.

▲ Part of the hornbill's beak is made of a horny material that has been compared with ivory. It is the only bird to produce this substance.

Rainforest Music

Trim-phones, smoke alarms, digital clocks . . . All the sounds of modern gadgets were invented by nature first!

To a musician, the rainforest is a magical place alive with curious sounds. You can tell what time of day it is by listening to the forest. In the early morning, among the symphony of sounds from near and far, gibbons whoop and warble in the canopy. A tiny bird sings a distinctive melody as if to say, 'Get up, it's half past six'.

One particular cicada, known at camp as the '6 o'clock cicada', whines like an electric sander shortly before sunset. Other birds, mammals and insects have their own distinctive sounds.

The rainforest is a perfect place to inspire new musical ideas – there are so many sounds: of cicadas, birds, owls, bats, bees, many more animals, the daily rain hammering down on us; even right through the night the noises never cease, especially the constant gushing of the river.

▲ Cicadas, the loudest of the insect singers, produce clicks by rattling the walls of their abdomens up to 600 times a second. The noise they make is so loud that a single insect can sometimes be heard a kilometre away!

◄ Tom was fascinated by the jungle sounds. In the early evening he could be seen at his favourite spot by the river playing his saxophone. The music he created captured the forest atmosphere. Tom says the rainforest will always be part of his music.

The Forest at Night

The trek to Wak Wak Camp takes about 2 hours at a good pace, but it involves a scramble up a 250 metre (800 ft) cliff. Another 1.5 km (1 mile) along a tree-covered ridge and you arrive at camp – a collection of wooden frames covered in tarpaulin.

Wak Wak (which means gibbon) is a field camp used by scientists working on the ridge. They don't use tents for sleeping out because they would be too hot. Instead, they make a 'pondok' – a wooden frame with stretchers across it, covered in tarpaulin to keep the rain off.

When Tom, Kieran and Severine arrived at Pondok Wak Wak they were totally exhausted from the

climb. The whine of the '6 o'clock cicada' told everyone that it would soon be dark. They collected wood to make a camp-fire.

By the glow of the fire Chris, the photographer, cooked a meal of spicy rice and vegetables. The smell of exotic cooking filled the night air. Looking up from the camp, there were no stars, just an unbroken ceiling of leaves.

▶ Flying squirrels are treetop denizens of night. They emerge from their nests at dusk to search for the fruits they eat.

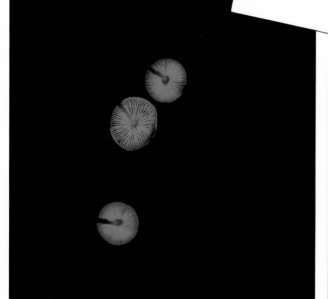

▲ Nature's streetlamps! During the midnight trek, Kieran spotted these curious glowing mushrooms which lit the team's way along the jungle trail.

▶ Huddled around the camp-fire, with the eerie sounds of the forest for company, Tom, Severine and Kieran taste Chris's exotic cooking as they prepare for a night sleeping out in the open.

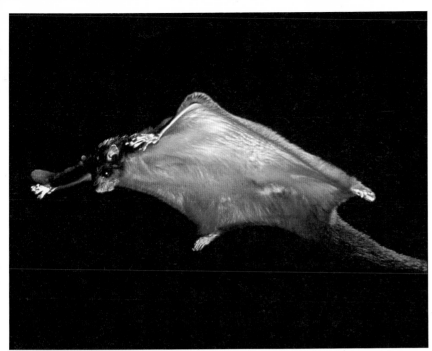

A Trek in the Dark

The team accompanied Dr Joe Charles as he searched for mammals in the night. He walked a few paces, waited silently, then shone a powerful, hand-held searchlight into the trees. He spotted a pair of glowing eyes looking down at him. The creature's head turned, then it swooped through the air and landed in a distant tree. Joe said it was a rare flying squirrel.

The team returned to camp and, after putting on lashings of insect repellent, settled down for the night. Despite hornets and snakes, the forest did not feel at all threatening. At night it is a peaceful place.

Magic Moments

The rainforest adventure wasn't all hard work. Between tough treks and whistle-stop tours of science projects, the expedition had its lighter side – mainly to do with the river!

Once Severine, Tom and Kieran realised that people were only joking about crocodiles and piranha fish, there was only one way for the three to cool off after a jungle trek: in the water! The river was gentle and refreshing and one of their favourite pastimes was to skim down the rapids with the current, trying not to graze their kneecaps on the pebbles.

Towards the end of the adventure the team had a chance to meet three young people from Brunei who were visiting the Centre. It was an interesting encounter because even though their homes are 11,265 km (7000 miles) apart they all had so much in common. It was also a chance to find out about each other's lives. Like Severine, Tom and Kieran, the Bruneians live in towns, they study the same subjects at school and, even though they live on the edge of the rainforest, this was their first journey into the wild interior.

Severine asked Rosalinda what she thought of the Batu Apoi rainforest. Rosalinda said she was surprised how rugged, beautiful and untouched it was. Now that she has seen the forest for herself, she would like to get involved with the research being carried out at Kuala Belalong when she leaves school. What would she do, asked Severine, if someone tried to cut down these forests? 'I would lie down in front of the bulldozers,' Rosalinda replied.

'The rainforest is the most magical place I have ever come across – in my eyes it really is one of the true wonders of the world. It has a constant, sparkling aura and is mystical and strange. One minute it feels just like home, the next it is creepy and far out.

It certainly did things to my mind – I fell completely in love with it and could have stayed longer. The 10 days in the jungle were 10 of the best days of my life. I think the whole experience changed me a lot. During my time there I became more aware of myself and what I am capable of – the forest made me feel more confident in life, as though I was conquering a fantastic challenge.'

Kieran

▶ The three young adventurers relax in the river that flows past the Kuala Belalong Field Centre. It was just one of the many 'magic moments' they enjoyed during their rainforest adventure.

▲ Kieran photographed with three young Bruneians who were visiting the Centre, and who shared his interest in rainforests.

'The rainforest is truly fantastic and not at all frightening – there are no lions or tigers, just bugs and lots of them! When it rained it poured, and the muddy paths were great to toboggan down. I really enjoyed swimming in the river and exploring the wilderness beyond.

Sleeping out in the open in the heart of the forest was an experience I'll never forget.

I couldn't understand why such wonders of nature are being destroyed by the hands of humans, so I was particularly heartened to meet some young people from Brunei who shared our interest.' *Severine*

▲ Chris, the photographer, takes a shot of Tom with a giant ant. (The ant is the one in the middle!)

'Before I went to Brunei I wanted to be a pilot in the RAF. I am still interested in this but I am not so set in my ambitions. I think the experience of being in the rainforest broadened my horizons. After living for two weeks with people who love the jungle and its animals I began to realise that the forest is much more important than everyone thinks. I am now interested in working in a rainforest with animals or trees, or maybe studying its hydraulics.

When I took my saxophone to the jungle I had great inspiration for music from all the weird and wonderful sounds made by its creatures.' *Tom*

▲ Severine wonders why her socks won't dry. Clothes can, in fact, stay damp literally for days in Brunei's hot and humid climate!

The Bukit at Sunset

Accompanied by a chorus of cicadas, the sun sets over Batu Apoi Forest Reserve. This is another view from the Bukit, the highest hill in the Reserve. The scene at dawn is shown on pages 24 and 25.

A Forest for the Future

Forests around the world are being cut down or burned to the ground faster than ever. About half of our planet's tropical forests have been felled over the last 20 years.

Trees are cut down for their hardwood (mainly for construction purposes or to make furniture or plywood sheets) or cleared so that the land can be used for grazing or growing crops for people. Fifty to 100 species, which have taken millions of years to evolve, may be lost every day. When trees are chopped down the land soon becomes useless. The soil is too poor to farm for long, so farmers have to move on to new forest lands.

International Co-operation

At the Earth Summit in Rio de Janeiro, Brazil, in June 1992, the leaders of many countries, including Britain, signed the Biodiversity Convention pledging to protect species throughout the world. It was not only a pledge for wildlife, it was a pledge for the future of planet Earth. By destroying the forests, we are not only killing millions of animals and plants, we are destroying the lungs of our planet.

It is easy for industrialised countries to turn to the inhabitants of the rainforests and tell them to stop the devastation now. But many poor people rely on logging, or farming on rainforest land, to make enough money to feed their families.

If we are to save the forests, and the people who depend on them, we must find alternative ways of using them so that we can benefit, long-term, from the riches of the rainforests without harming them.

The Way Forward

Amidst the devastation, the world is looking for a new way forward – to find ways of harvesting the rainforests for the benefit of mankind in a sustainable way.

This is why the Brunei Rainforest Project is so important. In April 1992, the Kuala Belalong Field Studies Centre was formally handed over to the University of Brunei Darussalam, under whose control it will continue as a permanent research station for rainforest scientists.

The work in Brunei's pristine jungle offers real hope for the future of rainforests all over the world.

▶ Lost forever. With no trees, the soil will soon lose its nutrients and become useless for growing. The forest cannot be replaced and farmers will soon have to move on and begin the destruction again. The only way to halt this kind of destruction is to find alternative ways of using the rainforest.

▶ The Batu Apoi Forest Reserve is a lighthouse of hope for all the world's rainforests. The research being carried out in this pristine jungle will help scientists to discover how to use rainforests to benefit mankind without destroying the forests.

Rainforest Action

The future of the world's rainforests is in our hands. Even though most of us live thousands of miles away from them, we can all play a part in helping to save them. One way to assess the impact our own lives have on the forests is to carry out an 'environmental audit'.

You and Your Environment

Start your audit by listing the products you and your family buy or use in your daily lives. Then find out which ones have a connection with rainforests.

A big object such as a wooden chair or a window frame may be made of rainforest timber, or the resin in the paint on your walls may have come from a rainforest tree. What about the food in your kitchen? Does it include bananas, cashew nuts or cocoa? These crops originally came from the forests but are now sustainably farmed for us all. Are you having a hamburger for lunch? If so, is there a rainforest connection? Where do the chemicals in the toiletries and cosmetics in your bathroom come from?

You can find out more by writing to companies about their products, and by contacting environmental groups like Friends of the Earth. Remember, the rainforest connection with your life isn't necessarily bad. If a product is harvested in a sustainable way – a way that doesn't use raw materials faster than nature can replace them –

we can benefit from the forests, without destroying them. Some suggestions are given here.

Use Your Power

Once you have made the rainforest connection, use your buying power to select environment-friendly products in supermarkets, cafés, do-it-yourself stores and furniture shops. You can discourage bad practice by refusing some products and choosing others – but be sure to tell the company why.

Consumer action does work. When children persuaded their parents not to buy aerosol sprays with CFC propellants that damage the ozone layer, within 5 years it was hard to find a shop that dared stock them.

Green consumerism has pressured companies and even governments to clean up their act.

How To Be a Friend of the Rainforest

■ Some companies produce cosmetics and toiletries from rainforest plants that have been grown and harvested in a sustainable way. Find out how the ones in your home are made. Exercise your buying power to encourage good practice.

■ Avoid buying products made from tropical hardwoods like mahogany and teak, unless it can be proved that the trees have been grown in a sustainable way. Hardwood is used for making furniture, window frames and plywood cladding.

■ The pen is mightier than the chain-saw! Write letters to newspapers, companies, Members of Parliament, and even the presidents of countries, telling them of your concerns. This will keep rainforest issues in the public eye. A well-thought-out enquiry, statement or complaint is a powerful tool in the battle to save the forests. It shows that people care.

■ Recycle it! Some raw materials, such as the aluminium used in drinks cans, are quarried from land that was once underneath tropical rainforests. By recycling aluminium cans you are reducing the need for more quarrying.

■ Before buying exotic house plants, find out where they come from. Many rainforest plants such as bromeliads, bird's nest ferns and orchids can be bought in garden centres and supermarkets. Most are cultivated in glasshouses, but some rare orchids are taken from the wild and are now endangered species. Check the label before you buy. Lobby supermarkets and garden centres to supply more information if there is any doubt about the plant's origin.

■ Be a Brazil-nut nut! Brazil nuts grow only in tropical rainforests because of their complicated pollination process involving insects and bats, and are harvested without damaging the forests. So don't just eat them at Christmas. By buying Brazil nuts you are helping local people make a living from the forest.

'I considered myself very ecological even before my visit to the rainforest. – I am a member of Friends of the Earth and I have always recycled everything from bottles to cans. I also always use public transport or walk whenever it is practical.

After being in Brunei I have become even more bossy towards my friends and family ecologically.'
Tom

'The experience of being in the rainforest changed my life and convinced me we must all do what we can to save the forests before it's too late.'
Severine

'It is easy to chop down a forest. Making proper use of its magic and produce is more difficult. It is important that people soon learn how to do this or we will lose one of Earth's great lifelines.'
Kieran

Useful Addresses

Here is a list of organisations to contact if you want further information. It is always a good idea to send a stamped, self-addressed envelope with your request.

Friends of the Earth
26–28 Underwood Street
London N1 7JQ
Campaigns throughout the world to protect the environment.

World Wide Fund for Nature
Panda House
Weyside Park
Godalming
Surrey GU7 1XR
Pressure group that funds schemes throughout the world.

The Rainforest Foundation
5 Fitzroy Lodge
The Grove
London N6 5JU
Organisation that specialises in rainforests and their original human inhabitants.

Survival International
310 Edgware Road
London W2 1DY
Campaigns to protect the inhabitants of rainforests and to increase their say in what happens to them.

Royal Geographical Society
1 Kensington Gore
London SW7 2AR
Major source of geographical information, and partners with the University of Brunei in the Brunei Rainforest Project.

International Council for Bird Preservation (ICBP)
32 Cambridge Road
Girton
Cambridge CB3 0PJ
Protects birds throughout the world

Index

Abu Salim, Dr Kamariah 38, 39
animal tracks and signs 51
ants 16, 34–5, 37
atmosphere 30

bamboo 13, 37
bananas 13, 26, 37
Bandar Seri Begawan (BSB) 18
Bangar 22
bats 16, 26, 62
Batu Apoi Reserve 8, 9, 10–11, 14–15, 24, 58–9
bears, Malayan sun 50, 51
bees 26
beetles 16, 26, 27, 29, 46
Belalong River 26
Bellamy, David 12, 13
Bernasconi, Severine 4–5, 11, 12, 13, 27, 31, 54, 57, 62
biodiversity 14, 60
birds 8, 9, 15, 32, 44, 46, 50, 51, 52–3
bomohs 38–9
Borneo 8, 9
branches 15, 16
Brunei Darussalam, University of 8, 10, 60
Brunei Rainforest Project 8
buhau trees 39
Bukit 24–5, 58–9
butterflies 8, 26, 27

Caldicott, Chris 47, 54, 57
camouflage 28, 31, 46, 47
canopy 8, 15, 16, 44–5, 50
carbon dioxide 30
caulifory habit 16–17
centipedes 46
Charles, Dr Joe 31, 55
Choy, Dr Satish 31
cicadas 26, 53, 54, 58
cichona trees 38
clothing 12, 26, 57
cobras 32, 33
cocoa 37
computer records 12, 31
conservation 30, 60–3
crabs 22, 31
Cranbrook, Lord 28
creepers 11, 16–17, 48–9
crocodiles 22
crops 30, 37, 60, 62

Darwin, Charles 9
Das, Dr Indraneil 32
dead trees 14, 16–17, 35, 36
deer, barking 33, 51
deforestation 40, 60
dehydration 28
dipterocarp trees 15, 40
diseases 12, 38–9
Dykes, Alan 26, 40

Earth Summit in Rio 60
environment 6, 26, 30, 62
epiphytic plants 15, 16, 44
Equator 14
erosion 26, 40, 60

ferns 8, 15, 36, 48–9, 62
fish 22, 31, 46
flower mantises 47
flowers 8, 36, 37
flying squirrels 50, 55
footwear 12, 26
forest floor 15, 16, 31, 38
frogs 32, 36, 44, 51
fruit 16, 20, 50
fungi 16, 36, 54

Geographical Information System 31
germination 15, 16
gibbons 50, 53
gingers 15

harvest 30, 37, 60, 62
Hebden, Kieran 4–5, 11, 12, 13, 18, 27, 29, 31, 38, 48–9, 54, 56, 62
Hewlett, Tom 4–5, 10, 12, 13, 31, 47, 53, 54, 57, 62
hornbills 8, 9, 50–1
hornets 55
house plants 62
houses, stilted 20

insect eating plants 36, 44
insects 8, 11, 12, 14, 16, 26, 27, 28, 29, 34–5, 36, 37, 44, 46, 47, 50, 51, 53, 54, 55, 58
ipecac plants 38

Kampong Ayer 20–1
Kew Gardens 6, 12, 13
kit 12
Kuala Belalong Field Studies Centre 8, 11, 26–7, 60

land clearance 30, 31, 40, 60
land erosion 26, 40, 60
landslides 40–1
laundry 26, 57
leaf litter 14, 35, 36, 51
leaves 13
leeches 11, 16
Levy, Ruth 26, 34, 35
light 8, 15, 16
lizards 26, 47, 50
loaches 31
logging 8, 30, 31, 60
Loya anak Kaling 39

mammals 31, 32, 44, 50, 51
    study of 31
mangrove swamps 22, 23
medicinal plants 30, 38–9
microbes 16
millipedes 26
monkeys 15, 22, 50
mosquito larvae 36
mucuna plants 39
mudflats 22
music 52–3

nutrients 16, 36, 60
nuts 62

oil wells 21
Omar Ali Saiffudin Mosque 18–19
orchids 8, 62
oxygen 23, 30

pitcher plants 36
plants 8, 14, 15, 16, 17, 36–7, 48–9
    useful 13, 30, 37, 38–9
pollination 16, 37, 62
pondoks 54
porcupines 51
potatoes 37
prawns 31
praying mantises 47
pythons 32, 33

quinine 38

rafflesia 8, 37
rain 12, 14, 16, 40, 44
Rainforest Adventure 10
rainforests: described 14
rapids 23, 30, 31
rattan palms (ant plants) 13, 35

recycling 16, 36, 62
rengas trees 16
rivers 22–3, 26, 31, 40
Royal Geographical Society 8, 10, 12

satellite navigation system 31
scientific studies 31, 44
scorpions 26
seasons 14, 36
seeds and seedlings 15, 16
sewerage works 26
silting 31
snakes 8, 15, 32–3, 44, 46, 55
soil, study of 40
soil erosion 26, 40, 60
sounds 50–3
South America 44
spiders 46, 47
squirrels 15, 50, 55
stick insects 26
strangler figs 16
sunlight 8, 15, 16
surveys, scientific 31, 44
swamps 22, 23

Temburong River 22–3, 40
termites 16, 35, 50
timber 8, 26, 27, 30, 31, 60, 62
transport 20, 22–3, 62
trees 14, 15, 16–17, 22, 23, 35, 36, 38, 39, 40, 44–5

undergrowth and understorey 16, 31

vaccinations 12
vines 8, 36, 37

Wak Wak Camp 54–5
Wales, HRH The Prince of 6
wasps' nests 44
water
    drinking 12, 28
    purification 26
    silting 31
    study of 40–1
    see also rain; rapids; rivers; waterfalls
waterfalls 28, 42–3
water villages 20–1
Wills, John 26, 31
wood 8, 26, 27, 30, 31, 60, 62
worms, mudcrunching 22

Picture credits:
BBC Books would like to thank the following for providing photographs and for permission to reproduce copyright material. While every effort has been made to trace and acknowledge all copyright holders, we would like to apologise should there have been any errors or omissions.
Apa Photo Agency pages 8 (Alain Compost), 35 (*right*, Larry Tackett), 37 (*top*, Larry Tackett) and 55 (*top*); **Ardea** pages 39 (*bottom*, Eric Lindgren), 50 (*left*, J.-P. Ferrero) and 53 (B. L. Sage); **Severine Bernasconi** page 56 (*bottom*); **Peter Brown** page 10–11; **Densey Clyne, Mantis Wildlife** pages 37 (*bottom*) and 47; **Bruce Coleman** pages 2 (Gerald Cubitt), 9 (*top*, C. B. Frith), 22 (*bottom*, D. and M. Plage), 26 (*left*, Gerald Cubitt), 27 (*bottom right*, Gerald Cubitt), 36–37 (Neyla Freeman), 50–51 (*top*, Alain Compost) and 54 (*left*, John Mackinnon); **Frank Lane Picture Agency** page 50 (*right*, M. Newman); **Tom Hewlett** page 57 (*right*); **Natural Science Photos** pages 3 (*bottom*) and 33 (*right*, Tony Davies-Patrick); **NHPA** page 9 (*bottom*, Morten Strange); **Oxford Scientific Films** pages 16 (*left*, N. M. Collins), 33 (*left*, Alastair Shay) and 60 (Charles Tyler); **K. G. Preston-Mafham** page 35 (*left*); **Shell UK Ltd** page 21 (*top*); **Frank Spooner/Gamma** page 44 (*left*, Raphael Gaillarde); **Survival Anglia** page 51 (*bottom*, Liz Bomford); **Patrick Thurston** pages 10 (*centre left*), 11 (*centre*) and 13; **Prof. David Warrell, Centre for Tropical Medicine, University of Oxford** page 46 (*left*).
The pictures on pages 10 (*left* and *right*), 11 (*right*) and 12 are **BBC copyright**, and all the remainder are by **Chris Caldicott/Royal Geographical Society**.